STREAMS
of Light

A Collection of Gospel Poems

EMMANUELLA NNEKA ARUKWE

Illustrated By: Mike Anim

To order additional copies of this book, contact:
Xlibris
844-714-8691
www.Xlibris.com
Orders@Xlibris.com

Library of Congress Control Number: 2022911503
ISBN: Softcover   978-1-6698-2717-7
         Hardcover   978-1-6698-2718-4
         EBook   978-1-6698-2716-0

Print information available on the last page

Rev. date: 07/07/2022

Acknowledgment

I especially acknowledge my friend, the Holy Spirit, who helped me create this work. I acknowledge my dad, the late Professor Emmanuel Nwanonye Obiechina, who instilled in me the love for words and built my confidence to write. I also acknowledge my sister, Nonye Obiechina Oke, whose poetic works inspired in me the desire to write a different genre of poetry.

I especially thank my publishing consultant, Isaac Armstrong, who conscientiously worked on this collection and motivated me to complete this work. God bless you abundantly.

Heartfelt thanks to my husband John and my children for your encouragement and support – you spur my dreams. Special thanks to God's able ministers whose teaching instilled faith and built my trust in God. May God reward you for teaching God's people His word. Appreciation to my numerous friends for your encouragement.

My sincere desire is that as you read through this collection of poems, light will burst forth, and you will be awakened unto Christ's love. I trust that you will be jolted, inspired, challenged, and encouraged to know Jesus Christ better and seek a deeper relationship with him for He is the essence of life.

Unstoppable

The devil loves to accuse
To tie me to his control;
Delighting in ripping my confidence,
He grips and tries obliterating my personality,
To subsume with a pseudo caricature.

He is a deft manipulator
Hitting and pounding at my weak areas;
Employing pulsating lies as his aces;
With a tenacious mirage of reality,
He poisons my thoughts and beliefs.

He disturbs my dreams, to cage my will,
Ensnaring me in confusion,
Leaving me to grope in the dark,
Wandering in circles, unhappy and forlorn,
A stranger within.

But Christ came and made the difference;
He has set me free;
Releasing me from chains of gripping bonds;
Encapsulating me with His love and power,
He has made me whole and wholesome.

I breathe the air of true freedom in Christ;
I know His love is real;
His watchful care certain;
His presence is solidity itself;
He never leaves nor forsakes me,
And I am free to be myself;
For He loves me for what I am - Me;
He sees all I am not;
He believes in who I can be,
For He knows what He made me to be.

I am dynamic;
Ready to explode to horizons unreached,
Drawing forth from the kingdom within;
Exploring my hidden treasures,
Unearthed, by Christ's liberation.

I can't be extinguished!
I can't be held back!
I sail through storms;
I soar through thick clouds;
For I'm made to conquer
That which seeks to hold me down.

Visions Unmarred

God open my eyes;
Let insight from within arise;
Let vileness be swallowed up
By the cleansing power of Christ's blood.

May I catch visions of heaven;
May heavenly melodies enthrall,
And rhapsodies delightfully fill my soul;
Lifting me to a realm of celestial bliss.

May I feel the power of Christ within,
Energizing me to the straight and narrow,
Removing the scales of callowness and callousness.

May I with piety come
Knowing that genuine repentance
Invokes His unending mercy;
May Christ's words captivate my soul;
May His lifestyle energize me;
May His spirit sustain me
To see the crown of righteousness;
The gold of life.

May I see vile substance
As vain shadows that fade away,
And may my visions remain clearly unmarred.

Eagles Unfettered

The carcass has been dumped;
Fallen, Forsaken, Fragmented;
Decomposing odors ooze out,
Polluting the atmosphere with stench;
Passers-by flee past with noses upturned,
Unwise to their own soul's disintegration.

The vultures hover,
Sniffing the air with relish;
Flapping in frenzied excitement;
Their dry, skinny necks rattle
As they behold the feast in sight.

And we, a brand of new men walk by
With zestful zeal burning in our hearts.

Arrested by stench and horror,
Our hearts are filled with compassion's milk;
Our legs are tied with lead;
But arrested by Christ's love,
Our new profession stirs us from within.

Even as we behold the scene,
Time appears suspended as fear grips our hearts,
And anxiety of contamination creeps into our heads;
With the fear of having little power to act,
Futility tries to cover us up;
But in this troubling darkness,
Light alights.

For within us lies the power of eagles to soar;
The power to give life to dead situations,
The power to preserve and restore the decomposing,
The power to call upon the name of Jesus Christ;
Faith with alertness grips our hearts;
Love from our heart flows,
Knowing that the dead are our brothers and sisters
Caught in the cruel game of life;
Sold to the merciless task masters – sin and slavery.

For we are eagles unearthed!
Called;
To give life to dead situations,
To preach to decaying corpses,
To minister to numbed flesh
Hardened by sin's deceit,
To announce the bishop of our souls
Who has birthed in us the spirit of God.

To our stupendous amazement,
Life to dead men, gradually returns,
As new flesh and sinews are supplied,
And a new breath is given to fragmented life;
For as eagles, we have indeed soared above
The pitiful situation;
Calling up a new breed of new saints for the
Bishop of our souls.

The vultures scurry hastily away
As the birthday miracle unfolds;
Scattering their ranks
And their expectations,
For eagles have been unearthed.

In the Dark Hours of the Night

In the dark hours of the night,
When sorrow and pain etch deep;
When cries from troubled souls erupt;
When tears know no respite;
You gently tip-toe in.

In the nights of strange shadows,
When the brave, is fear engraved,
When danger roams unfettered,
Your presence makes daylight of dreaded night.

Christ, you are the panacea to fear;
Your light envelopes us;
Your light scatters darkness;
For God has commanded light to shine out of darkness.

Deceit

The devil does not come ugly;
He has no horns or tail;
He is not black decked;
He is no dark shadow or gruesome beast.

He comes in the pricey garment of religion;
Seemingly near to God, yet afar off;
He comes dazzling in sparkling light,
With radiating warmth and sunshine,
But completely embedded in cold;
He comes like a luscious apple,
Teeming with maggots.

For deceit is the name of his game;
He creeps in so gently,
But grips so tenaciously.

Vice he strews around,
In the guise of pleasure;
Promising a Utopia
To trap the unwary soul
In hell's coven.

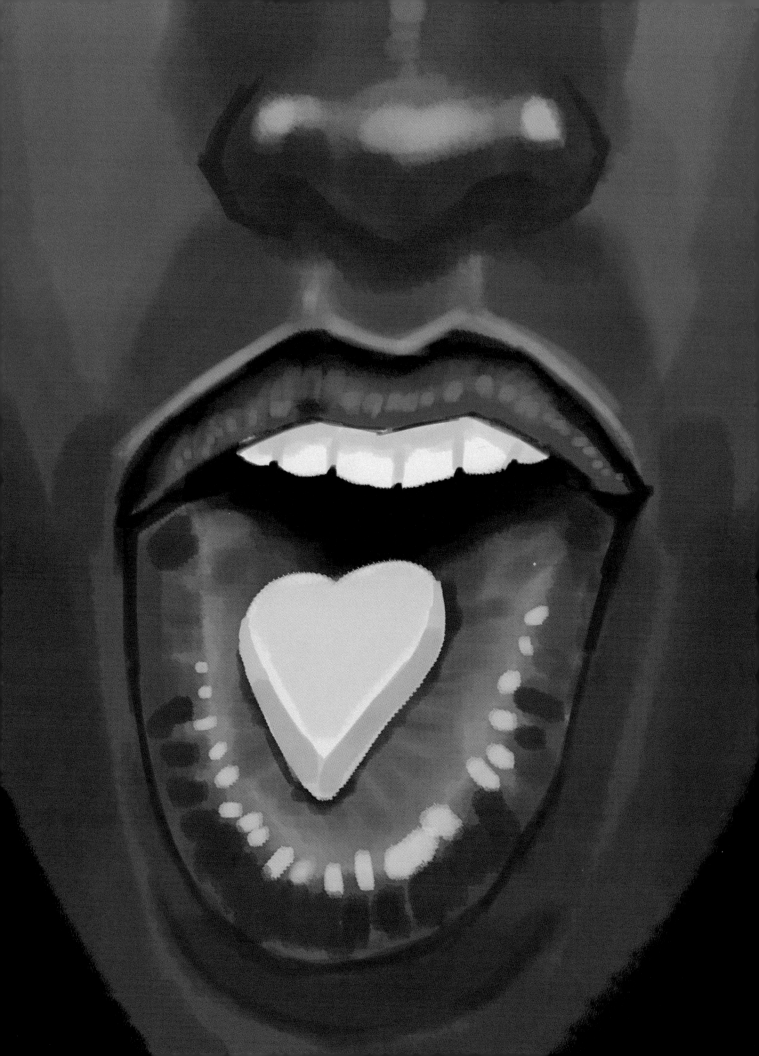

My Tongue

My tongue is a gift from God;
It is a glowing piercing rod
With which I pitch a fall,
As it sends a praise call;
My tongue I must learn to check
Or it could make me a wreck;
Lies it should not tell,
For lies pave a way to hell.

Christ it must always preach,
For that's the truth to reach;
Evil it must never speak,
For it drags me from a peak.

Gossip it must never spread,
For it hinders progress ahead;
Faith it should always express,
For that's an antidote to stress.

God's word it should always say,
To release the blessings of the day.

Juxtaposition

In the enigma called man,
Good and evil appear embodied;
Cohabiting in this mortal frame,
Seemingly enmeshed in a struggle for domination.

And man is encapsulated within,
As he swings with frenzied dance steps;
Dancing to the perceived stronger rhythm,
As juxtaposition holds sway.

The evil he abhors, he does;
The good he desires, he chokes;
And chameleon-like, he appears,
As reflections and refraction from him emerge.

Man seems at sea within,
As schizophrenic he lives;
Unsure of who he really is,
Till the reality of Christ's
Death unfolds to him;
For man was not meant
To be dominated by divergent forces.

For Christ by His death emptied out inhibiting fears;
Holding the key to unlock juxtaposition;
Emboldening us with embedded powers;
Liberating powers from God.

For juxtaposition, resurrection did destroy,
Leaving us masters of our fate;
For the power of righteousness has been bestowed,
And we can do all things through Christ Jesus.

They Tell it as it is

They tell it as it is
For that's the way they are;
For guile has not beguiled them,
Neither has tact tricked them,
Nor expedience enslaved them.

Children are as plain as boiled white yam;
Unmixed with the slipperiness of oil;
Not spiced with condiments and spices,
Nor garnished with vegetable dressing.

Childish we scream,
But chide-less they are;
And in a world full of double speak,
They provide the facts,
As they tell it, tongue unchecked.

A Child's Reminiscence

Oh God! Today is Sunday,
But sunny days appear at bay;
We cannot have rice to eat;
Mother says it is a treat.

Prices of goods sky rocket;
Holes have invaded pockets;
And we have to drink pap;
Mother says it fills the gap.

Oh God! Our parents appear sapped dry;
We children cannot help but cry;
We long wistfully for past years,
As the past is extolled in our ears.

Sighs seem our habitual uttering,
For we see our elders often muttering;
Frowns and furrow seem etched on faces;
They all seem like photo traces.

Oh Lord! Save our country from doom;
For we perceive an atmosphere of gloom;
Your divine intervention we call down,
For only you can erase our frowns.

Good leaders we pray for,
To lift the plight of the poor;
Truth and justice, we desire,
To become our nation's life wire.

Hope we embrace,
As we pray down God's grace;
For we foresee a new nation
With righteousness as the bastion,
And salvation bells ringing forth,
Increasing our national worth.

Rebirth

I am born again;
A cleansing has taken place;
The chain of sin removed;
The garment of filth discarded;
My old nature is gone;
And I step out soaring;
For God has added extra to my ordinary life;
I have become extraordinary;
God has put super to my natural self;
I am supernatural;
God has added value to my ability;
I am valuable;
I have been recreated;
I am a new brand;
Displaying a newness of life.

Thanksgiving

Dear God,
Thank you for bestowing on me
The beauty and loveliness of Esther,
The wisdom of Solomon,
The prayer life of Elijah,
The fierceness of John the Baptist,
The excellence of Daniel,
The favor of Israel,
The faithfulness of Ruth,
The steadfastness of Job,
The blessings of Joseph,
The zeal of Peter,
The faith and obedience of Abraham,
The meekness of Moses,
The submissiveness of Sarah,
The grace of Mary,
The communion of Enoch,
The longevity of Methuselah,
The youthfulness of Caleb,
The love of Jonathan,
The good works of Dorcas,
The heart of David,
The might of Samson,
The courage of Deborah,
And the wholeness of Jesus Christ.

Procrastination

Procrastination, a fifteen-letter mouthful;
Intimidating in number,
And destabilizing in effect.

Procrastination, you prowl about my life;
Snuffling life from my visions,
Incapacitating my energies,
Strewing wasted talents around
As you ungalvanized my strength.

You benumb me with lethargy;
And zest is slowly drained away,
As I stand apathetic,
Unfulfilled, drained, and unhappy.

You crept into my life
And enthroned mediocrity;
You stole my precious time;
Leaving my targets out of tangent.

In the seeming quagmire,
I realize procrastination is a negative experience,
Giving me a distorted order;
And now I take stock of my life knowing I have
The power to curb its flow.

I masterfully take hold of my life,
Preserving each hour for God's blessing,
Seeing time as God's precious gift to me.

I allow His breath to energize me;
And I learn His will is the plus
Needed to break procrastination's backbone;
And now I redeem the time.

Prayer of the Hour

Oh God You are my Lord;
You are my life's keeper;
Tie me to you with a cord;
Let bonds of love with you grow deeper.

May I see you as you are;
With eyes uncolored by fear,
So I can trust in your care
And your love so dear.

May I with a childlike faith, believe;
That Jesus on the cross, sin did nail;
So sin's lies will no longer deceive;
And I can live a life without sin's trail.

May I, my strength and weakness bring,
And know that all is but dross;
And unto your feet do both fling,
So I can cling to Christ's cross.

Millennium Bug

The bug has caught on;
Y2K - Yes to Christ, Yes to Kingdom;
Excitement crawls and anticipation skips,
As a new dawn quietly draws closer;
For an era quickly departs,
And a new millennium is born.

Acclamations and shouts resound,
As gun shots rent the air;
The fear of the devil is out of our sphere,
As we fix our gazes on the glorious one;
Contemplating the splendor of His radiance
And His imminent return.

We know for certain
That the future of the church beckons;
That the Church, with abated breath gasps;
For a glorious era dawns;
An era of Christ's majestic glory
Unleashed in increased proportions.

The Knock

A knock at my heart's door is heard;
I have heard many knocks before;
Gate-crashing knocks, Intruding knocks,
Soul stealing knocks,
And I have been knocked out by knocks before;
This knock was different, it had a consistent rhythm;
Gentle, yet steadfast,
With pressure, at my heart's door.

I brushed it aside but the knock was persistent;
Reverberating hard against my soul;
I need to answer, cannot ignore;
That precious call, I alone can hear;
Promises of hope, fulfillment, and joy;
The call to salvation;
Praise God for that knock
On the gate of my soul.

I open the door
And a gush of peace
Envelopes my heart;
Warmth and wholesomeness pervade me,
For Christ has walked in.

Who is He?

Controversy is stirred;
Tempers are flared;
As the resounding question reverberates:
"Who is He?"

To some a prophet, others a teacher;
To some a mystic, others a miracle worker;
But one fact stands out;
Jesus walked the earth,
And his short life still impacts the earth
Because he etched his feet
On eternity's roll of honor.

He proclaimed to be God;
He claimed to be life's bread;
He claimed to be living water;
He claimed to be the way, the truth, and the light;
He claimed to be the vine and the door.

Miracles He strewed around;
Love He personified;
Breaking barriers and boundaries;
Compassion oozed out of him,
And wisdom from His lips, gushed.

Promises He was never afraid to make;
Peace, rest, and satisfaction He bestows;
Everlasting and abundant life He promises.

Belief in His name transforms lives,
Emboldens crawling cringing cowards,
Changes filthy habits,
Energizes tired souls,
Heals broken bodies,
Restores destroyed dreams.

And as the controversy shimmers,
One solution unveils itself;
Taste and see that He is the Lord God Almighty.

Lovely But Free

Money, the answer to man's quest they think,
As man and woman, misguided,
Fall and worship at its feet;
Trapped in the futility of their mind's delusion,
That greater money leads to a better life.Unknown to them, a wondrous God of love
Has freely bestowed on us lovely things to enjoy;
The warmth of the sun,
The coolness of the breeze,
The beauty of the flowers,
The majesty of the clouds,
The therapeutic effect of laughter,
The refreshingness of sleep,
The relief of tears,
The freshness of water,
The lushness of the meadows,
The lightness of a good conscience,
Salvation in the blood of Jesus,
The gift of the Holy Spirit,
And true riches in Christ.

A Journey Through the Book

I am on a journey;
Rummaging on wondrous discoveries
As I undertake a New Testament search,
Unearthing treasures:
I march up with Mathew;
I mark well with Mark;
I look intently at the book of Luke;
I join the expeditions in John;
I act out the acts of the Apostles;
I ruminate on Romans;
I am corrected by Corinthians
I am galvanized by Galatians;
I am made effective by Ephesians;
I am fulfilled by Philippians;
My life is colored by Colossians;
I am tested by Thessalonians;
I am tamed by Timothy;
I am tutored by Titus;
I am fortified by Philemon;
I am helped by Hebrew;
I am jolted by James;
I am prepared by Peter;
I am judged by Jude;
I journey through 1st, 2nd and 3rd John;
My future is revealed in Revelation;
And I come out refired and reinvigorated;
Basking in the beauty of unearthed riches;
My life is enriched and ennobled,
As The Book transforms me.

Complete in Him

Here she stands;
Complete in Him;
Resplendent to behold;
Clothed with the garment of salvation;
Robed in the robe of righteousness;
Adorned with the priceless ornaments
Of a meek and quiet spirit;
Crowned with the crown of glory;
She stands with her feet shod
With the Gospel of Peace;
Perfumed with the fragrance of good works;
Enveloped in God's unending love;
Encompassed by the gates of praise,
As she stands complete in Him;
Birthed by His spirit;
Awakened to newness of life.

Transformation

Here He comes;
Ever so gentle;
Compelling with deft ease;
As He changes the lives He touches,
The stories abound.

A grabbing prostitute becomes
A generous giver,
As the precious bottle of alabaster oil is broken.

An unstable fisherman
Becomes solidarity itself;
Unshaken in this earth's shaking conviction
On the Lordship of Christ.

A zealous murderer
Is arrested by Him,
And becomes a love slave;
Completely sold out to Him.

A greedy cheat
Repents of his ill-gotten gains,
And stoops to restore
And bless suffering lives.

For Christ touches to the root;
Cleanses downright out
With his loving touch;
And transformation unfolds.

Shipping

I undertake a voyage with God
As I go shipping;
I enter into a relationship
As I acknowledge His Lordship and my sonship;
I bask in worship and enjoy fellowship;
It becomes like a courtship
And develops into a partnership
As I submit to His leadership;
It is more than membership and flagship;
As I stay connected to Him,
I am shipped into shape.

Affirmation

I seek affirmation;
Searching for an identity within;
Struggling for self-worth
As futility fervently flutters my flight.

I notice the ugly sneer of the naysayers,
As contemptuously they dismiss me;
Weighing me in their convoluted balance
And concluding I am feather weight.

I hear the smirk of the self-righteous
As they feed their grandiose delusions,
And disdainfully upturn their noses and utter dartful words
At my faltering steps.

I taste the bitter pills of past mistakes
Leaving an aftertaste of stale dreams;
I soliloquize as the past shadow looms
And the present becomes a tale of happenstance,
While the future appears like a cloud of benumbed actions.

I am bereft of an identity;
Circumventing as my attempts at self-definition deflate me;
In confounding confusion, I cry out to my maker:
"Who really am I?"

Silence! Succor! Solution!
The Manual!! The answer in my heart is softly breathed;
Search therein and find yourself;
I stand excitedly as hope sways me forward and the lessons begin.

Voraciously I devour the manual – God's gift for life;
Answers gush forth as understanding is birthed;
My life's worth is wrapped up in Jesus Christ
Who enlightens every one who comes to Him.

Because He is, I am;
Because He lives, I live;
I can do because He does.

I come forth refreshed, refined and reinvigorated;
Knowing that my identity is in Him,
For I have been affirmed in Him.

The Canvas

I stare at the canvas
Strewed forth with vibrant colors,
Telling forth the story of a work in progress;
I might not understand the painting,
The concept may appear abstract,
The colors may appear discordant,
The painting seeming to lack beauty,
But I am not the artist;
And the painter patiently polishes His work.

As the project nears completion,
Discordant colors seem to blend in;
Rough edges smoothened out;
A symmetry runs through the painting
Showing divergent ebbs and flows,
And I gape at a beautiful painting;
Displaying the dexterity and artistry of the master painter – God;
For from different paints strewed on the canvas,
A master piece has been created.

Dressing Up and Down Dressing

Looking good is good business, the cliché reads;
As fashion bluffs blaze the trail;
As they are resplendently arrayed
And admiration from a besotted audience expressed.

A fashion hit is all about good dress sense, carriage,
And avoiding fashion mishaps they say;
Sartorial dressing is the ace;
I stand in the throngs reflecting on those myriads of books, magazines, articles and shows
That deal with proper physical dressing,
While spiritual dressing with eternal value is deliberately ignored.

I contemplate that the master creative artist – Almighty God,
Liberally bestowed on us spiritual fashion insight;
Left instructions in the book to make us spiritually glorious and beautiful;
I carefully ponder the instructions and I start the act
Of dressing up and dressing down.

I put on Christ;
I put on the new man;
I put on the whole armor of God;
I put on the garments of praise;
I put on the robe of righteousness;
I put on the ornaments of a meek and quiet spirit;
I put on bowels of mercies;
I put on kindness and humbleness of mind;
I put on meekness and longsuffering;
I put on love.

I take off the old man with his deeds;
I put off lies and vain speaking;
I put off malice and hypocrisy;
I put off anger and wrath;
I put off blasphemy and filthy conversation.

I stand tall, beautiful, and exalted;
Depicting true and unfading beauty,
As my fashion sense has essence,
And I step out with my feet shod with the Gospel
To turn fashion bluffs into spiritual nerds.

Eternity in My Heart

Men and women
Rustle, bustle, and scuttle around,
Searching for illusive power and longevity.

Deluded in their minds' eyes
As they seek out the knowledge of the ancients;
Mesmerized with the illusion of deep hidden truths
That transcends mortality.

Drowning in longevity potions and concoctions;
Searching fruitlessly for a panacea to death;
Ignorant of the knowledge of truth
That Christ has demystified death;
As He freely gives to those who truly believe and proclaim
Eternity in their hearts.

Shouts of joy and exhilaration from me gushes
As I experience the truth of His words;
That the kingdom of God is within me;
As in the new birth,
God sets eternity in my heart.

Out of my heart flows
Rivers of living waters;
My heart holds the issues of life;
I store up treasures in my heart;
And out of the abundance of my heart
My mouth speaks.

A new melody is heard;
A new song is sung;
A new language is learnt;
I am indestructible;
I am unquenchable;And I live eternally as
Eternity lives in my heart.

Full Life

My life in Christ Jesus is full;
His infinite love makes me grateful;
His loving care makes me thankful;
His everlasting compassion makes me thoughtful;
His unending grace makes me merciful;
His encompassing wisdom makes me resourceful;
His mighty strength makes me powerful;
His radiant glory makes me beautiful;
His tenderness makes me helpful;
His enveloping presence makes me cheerful;
His resounding victory makes me successful;
His abiding trust makes me truthful;
So I enjoy a life that is blissful
And a cup that is overly full.

Sands of Time

He walked the earth;
His feet etched in the sands of time;
He shook the earth and disquieted the heavens
From cradle to saddle;
His life strewed history's pages.

Words no man ever did speak,
From him proceeded forth;
Wisdom paradoxically displayed,
As his words blessed the simple and confounded the wise.

tg x/2 = 1 − cos x / sin x = sin x / 1 + cos x = √(1 − cos x / 1 + cos x)
cos 2x = cos²x − sin²x
1000000 * 0 = 0

Zero Level

I play around with numeracy
As I try to figure out Mathematics;
Logic and rationality seem entwined in formulas and deductions.

I debate, muse, and soliloquize on how scientific Mathematics is;
The omnibus term *'ceteris paribus'* jars my reflections;
I ponder on the probability that all things will be equal;
In this contemplative state, questions float in my mind.

The absurdity that trillions multiplied by zero results in zero, perplexes me;
As I affirm that hyperbole is mathematical,
New insights are fueled and unfold
In these seeming distortions.

The words of the master resound in my spirit;
As I recollect that Jesus enunciated the principle
In simple and enduring truth;
That without Christ we can do nothing.

The truthful ramification of the assertion crystallizes in my heart;
That all achievements or gains
That are not Christ centered, breathed, birthed, or enabled,
Is but dross, of no eternal value, of zero level;
A mirage without substance;
A tottering shadow
That disintegrates leaving embers of nothingness.

Paradox

The Bible is a book of books;
To make the simple wise and to show forth the folly of the wise;
Paradox it sounds but paradoxical it is.

Poetry and prose have free expression;
As the pages are combed,
Insight is granted to babes and the childlike,
Whilst the wise are confounded;
Hidden truths are paradoxically unveiled.

It affirms that to gain our life we have to lose it;
The first shall be the last and the last first – it proclaims;
Seeing, some do not see, and hearing, some do not hear – it cautions;
A thousand years is like a day, and a day is a thousand years to God – it declares.

As we prayerfully study to show ourselves approved of God,
The author of the book, the Holy Spirit, enunciates paradoxes;
And understanding becomes fruitful,
As the letter killeth but the spirit giveth life,
And hidden truths are unveiled.

In the Volume of the Book

In the volume of the book I come;
My life is no accident or fluke;
I am not a mystery mystified;
My life is not a puzzle to be unraveled.

For I walk in preordained paths,
Fulfilling predestined causes;
Walking and living my life's story;
Navigating the twists and turns of the story.

It is an exhilarating adventure,
As the end in mind is my fixation;
Knowing that all things work together for my good;
For I love God and I am called according to His purpose.

My purpose beckons, and I step out as the light of the world,
The salt of the earth, a city set on a hill that cannot be hidden;
A savior in Zion, preordained to display good works;
Populating heaven and depopulating hell.

I am on stage, displaying glory and virtues;
Acting out my script under the directorship of the Holy Spirit,
And the crowds of glory as bystanders, cheer me on.

Demystified

Life is a mystery – men muse;
God is unfathomable – they enthuse;
We are pawns in the game – they cry;
Destiny roams rampage – leaving us dry.

Excuses become our play toy;
Goading inaction is the ploy;
Creativity is emasculated and torn;
And dreams are stillborn;
Lo, hidden truth is revealed,
As the beauty of life is unveiled;
For Christ in us is the hope of glory,
And His life within sets another story;
Vigor is invigorated with speed,
As lying barriers we do not heed;
Knowing that we hold the aces
As we embark on life's races.

Trading Places

I sit contemplative,
Reflecting on true love;
Noting that it is unseen in gushing words,
Nor in emotive lyrics fueled by unbridled passions,
For love is action displayed;
Gratitude from my heart ebbs forth
To the one who truly loves us profusely;
For Christ is love personified,
Because He traded places.

He died for me to live;
Became sin to establish my righteousness;
Bore sickness to provide my health;
Made poor to bequeath me riches;
Crowned with thorns to crown me with glory;
Gave me beauty for ashes;
Replaced a spirit of heaviness with a garment of praise.

I am accepted in the beloved;
I dance with melody in my heart,
Celebrating Christ's compassion with passion;
For greater love hath no one
Than Christ who paid it all
When He traded places.

Detoxification

In the bustle and hustle of fast paced life,
I eat a junk diet;
Jaundiced news,
Fear mongering,
And Juicy Gossip;
Constipation is the aftermath,
And I grapple with pain;
Pushing me to detoxify my body;
I drink in the Word of God,
Meditate on its truth,
Affirm its veracity,
And bask in its light;
A cleansing has begun,
Old diets discarded,
New diets begin,
As I learn to eat the wholesome Word of God;
I feel a new freshness and energy,
And I resolve to consistently detoxify myself
With the abiding Word of God.

Lit Up

The Word of God is my light,
Giving me uncommon insight;
It dispels the darkness of night;
It is my Soul's delight.

It energizes me with might,
Scurrying fear to hurried flight;
I win the faith fight
And shine so bright.

It delivers my birthright,
And helps me walk upright;
It beams its search light
And heralds me into limelight.

It restores the blind to sight
And repairs eyesight;
It turns midnight to moonlight
And makes the day blaze sunlight.

Reconstruction

God created man in his image,
With a divine destiny in Christ Jesus;
Man, through the ages seeks to reconstruct God;
Uncomfortable with the God they are accountable to,
Deluded to create in their mind's futility,
A pseudo god of relativism,
As they define God from their perspective;
Refusing to acknowledge the sovereignty of God
Despite the manifold evidences nature displays;
As they choose to worship and serve the created,
Rather than seek to serve the Almighty Creator;
Alas man is confused!
As lust, sin, guilt, restlessness, and despair overwhelm him,
For man was made to commune with God;
To enjoy and serve God in love;
But a pseudo god cannot satisfy him,
For God knows what is best for man;
As true joy, peace, and fulfillment comes
Only when man to his Creator submits;
For God reconstructs a willing man
And lifts him from mortality to immortality;
As man yields his life to God,
A new birth is birthed,
And man is crowned with glory.

Best Shot

It is important that whatever happens you give your life to Christ and enjoy all the blessings in Him. If you are yet to be Born Again, please pray aloud the Salvation Prayer below.

Salvation Prayer

Oh Lord God, I thank you for sending your Son Jesus Christ to come to earth and to die for my sins. I thank you that when He died, He was buried and God you raised Christ from the dead for my justification. I confess with my mouth that Jesus Christ is the Lord of my life. I receive by faith eternal life into my heart. Jesus Christ is my Lord and Saviour. I am *Born Again*. Thank you, Father, for Salvation.

Printed in the United States
by Baker & Taylor Publisher Services